DAV PILKEY
RISE

How a Creative Genius Conquered Children's Literature

Earl B. Holman

All rights reserved. No part of this publication may be reproduced, distributed, or transmitted in any form or by any means, including photocopying, recording, or other electronic or mechanical methods, without the prior written permission of the publisher, except in the case of brief quotations embodied in critical reviews and certain other noncommercial uses permitted by copyright law.

Copyright © (**Earl B. Holman**), (2025)

Table of Contents

- INTRODUCTION..3
- CHAPTER 1..13
  - Early Years and Childhood.....................................13
- CHAPTER 2..22
  - School Struggle and Early Inspiration....................22
- CHAPTER 3..32
  - College Years and the Path to Becoming An Author..32
- CHAPTER 4..42
  - A Breakthrough for Captain Underpants................42
- CHAPTER 5..52
  - Overcoming Obstacles in the Publishing Industry..52
- CHAPTER 6..62
  - Expanding the Pilkey Universe...............................62
- CHAPTER 7..72
  - Personal Life and Inspiration..................................72
- CHAPTER 8..83
  - Dav Pilkey's Legacy and Enduring Impact.............83
- CONCLUSION..94
- APPENDIX..99

INTRODUCTION

Dav Pilkey is more than a best-selling author; he is a literary revolutionary who has changed the way children interact with books. His personal journey from a struggling student with ADHD and dyslexia to one of the world's best-known children's authors is both inspiring and profound. Pilkey's life story speaks to countless children who face similar academic and personal challenges, demonstrating that unconventional thinkers and dreamers can thrive despite adversity.

Pilkey's academic struggles could have had a negative impact on his life. He struggled in traditional learning environments due to his ADHD and dyslexia diagnosis. Teachers misunderstood him, peers mocked him, and he was frequently disciplined for his excessive energy and creativity. Rather than allowing these difficulties to silence him, Pilkey found an outlet through drawing and storytelling. He started sketching funny comic-style characters in class, which would eventually lay the groundwork for his literary career.

His story is important because it provides hope and encouragement to children who feel like misfits. The traditional education system can sometimes discourage creative thinkers who do not fit into rigid structures. Pilkey's success demonstrates that intelligence and creativity come in various forms. His books are now read by millions of people around the world, and his story continues to inspire young readers and aspiring writers who might otherwise believe that their struggles define their future.

Pilkey's story is noteworthy not only for his personal perseverance, but also for the way he transformed children's literature. He didn't just write books; he reinvented the reading experience for children, making stories more engaging, accessible, and enjoyable. Pilkey dared to defy the conventions of children's publishing by emphasizing humor, unconventional storytelling, and a thorough understanding of how children think. He recognized early on that many children, particularly reluctant readers, struggled with traditional literature. Instead of forcing them into rigid literary structures, he met them where they were by providing fast-paced, action-packed, and laugh-out-loud funny stories with engaging illustrations.

Another reason his story is relevant is his commitment to inclusivity. Pilkey never intended to write books solely for academically gifted children. Instead, he wrote for the child who doodles in class, the child who finds traditional books boring, and the young reader who has difficulty reading long paragraphs. He wrote his stories with humor and illustrations that appealed to even the most reluctant readers, ensuring that every child had the opportunity to enjoy reading. His books are meant to be picked up and enjoyed by anyone, regardless of reading ability.

Furthermore, Pilkey's personal experiences with rejection and censorship emphasize the importance of adhering to one's creative vision. Many of his books, particularly "Captain Underpants", have been banned and criticized due to their humor, language, and irreverent tone. However, he never compromised his vision, believing that children deserve books that make them laugh, inspire their creativity, and celebrate their uniqueness. His tenacity in the face of controversy sends a powerful message, encouraging young people to embrace their distinct voices and trust their instincts, even when the world pushes back.

Pilkey's journey has taught children valuable life lessons about perseverance, self-acceptance, and the power of creativity, in addition to providing them with entertaining books. His story is important because it demonstrates that success is not limited to those who fit into conventional molds. It belongs to the dreamers, outcasts, and those who dare to think differently.

His Influence on Children's Literature

Dav Pilkey's contribution to children's literature is nothing short of revolutionary. He has transformed children's reading experiences, bridging the gap between reluctant readers and the joy of storytelling. Before Pilkey, children's books frequently followed traditional structures, with long paragraphs, moral-heavy narratives, and a clear distinction between picture books and novels. Pilkey defied these expectations, demonstrating that books could be as hilarious, visually engaging, and immersive as comic books or cartoons.

His most famous creation, "Captain Underpants", defied all conventional rules. With its absurd humor, flipbook action sequences (Flip-O-Rama), and fourth-wall-breaking style, the series was unlike anything else seen in children's literature. Pilkey recognized that children wanted stories that made them laugh, and he delivered outrageous characters, hilarious dialogue, and action-packed adventures. He transformed reading into an experience, not a chore or an academic requirement, but a source of pure pleasure.

One of Pilkey's most significant contributions is his ability to engage reluctant readers. Many children struggle with traditional books because of the long text, complicated vocabulary, or dry storytelling. Pilkey's use of comics, illustrations, and playful language helps to bridge the gap, making reading more accessible and enjoyable. By combining drawings and words, he develops a visual storytelling method that keeps children engaged. His books serve as a starting point for many young readers, inspiring them to develop a lifelong love of reading.

Pilkey's work also made significant contributions in terms of normalizing and celebrating children's creativity. Many of his protagonists—such as George and Harold in "Captain Underpants" and Li'l Petey in "Dog Man"—are young, imaginative children who write their own comic books. This reflects Pilkey's real-life childhood, when he found solace in drawing at school. Pilkey sends a powerful message by making creativity the central theme of his stories: storytelling is for everyone, not just adults or professional authors. His books encourage children to draw, write, and express themselves freely, resulting in a wave of young fans creating their own comics and stories.

Pilkey has also addressed important themes in a way that appeals to young readers. His "Dog Man" series, for example, delves into complex themes such as redemption, kindness, and the value of second chances, all while maintaining the humor and excitement that children enjoy. Pilkey subtly teaches readers valuable lessons about growth, forgiveness, and personal transformation through characters such as Petey the Cat, who starts out as a villain but eventually changes. These deeper messages add layers of meaning to his books, elevating them beyond mere entertainment to become sources of inspiration and education.

Furthermore, Pilkey's influence transcends the pages of his books. He has become an advocate for children's literacy, frequently participating in book tours, school visits, and other events that encourage children to enjoy reading and creativity. His approachable personality and personal story make him a relatable role model for young readers. He frequently speaks openly about his struggles with ADHD and dyslexia, thereby helping to dispel misconceptions about learning disabilities and demonstrating to children that being different is not a weakness, but rather a strength.

His influence extends to the publishing industry as well. Pilkey's success has opened the door for more graphic novels and illustrated chapter books in children's literature. In recent years, there has been an increase in hybrid formats that combine text and illustrations, inspired by Pilkey's distinctive storytelling style. Authors like Jeff Kinney ("Diary of a Wimpy Kid") and Lincoln Peirce ("Big Nate") have followed in his footsteps, writing books that appeal to a similar audience. Pilkey's contributions have helped to shape children's literature into something more inclusive, visually appealing, and welcoming to all types of readers.

Beyond the books, Pilkey's works have been adapted into films, television series, and merchandise, broadening his audience and influence. The 2017 "Captain Underpants: The First Epic Movie" demonstrated his storytelling's universal appeal by bringing his characters to life on the big screen and introducing them to a larger audience. The "Dog Man" series is also slated for adaptation, cementing Pilkey's status as one of the most influential figures in children's literature today.

Dav Pilkey's contribution to children's literature cannot be overstated. He has redefined what makes a book appealing to children, promoted creativity, and made reading enjoyable for millions of people. His books are more than just stories; they are experiences that sparked imagination, laughter, and a lifelong passion for reading. Through his work, he has altered the landscape of children's publishing, demonstrating that humor, creativity, and a thorough understanding of young readers can produce literary magic. His legacy will continue to inspire future generations of children to value books, storytelling, and the limitless potential of their own imaginations.

CHAPTER 1

Early Years and Childhood

Dav Pilkey was born on March 4, 1966, in Cleveland, Ohio, and raised in a loving yet challenging environment. The Pilkey family was close-knit, with parents who encouraged their children despite the difficulties they faced. Dav's father worked as a steel salesman, and his mother was a homemaker who fostered his early creativity. Despite having a supportive family, Dav's childhood was far from easy.

Pilkey had boundless energy from a young age, making him a nuisance at home and school. His Ohio neighborhood was a typical suburban setting, with children playing outside, riding bikes, and using their imaginations. Pilkey, on the other hand, struggled to fit into the school system, whereas other children appeared to glide right in. School, which was supposed to be a place of learning and development, quickly turned into a battleground for him.

His early years in school were difficult, due in large part to his learning disabilities. Teachers expected students to sit still, follow instructions, and finish assignments neatly and on time. Unfortunately, these were the things that Pilkey found nearly impossible to accomplish. He struggled to focus, couldn't sit still for long, and found reading and writing extremely frustrating. This made him stand out from his peers, often in ways that attracted negative attention.

Despite these obstacles, Pilkey's childhood in Ohio shaped him in ways he could not have predicted at the time. The difficulties he faced in school pushed him toward the creative outlet that would one day define his career. His experiences as a restless, misunderstood child laid the groundwork for the wit, relatability, and rebellious spirit that would later make his books so popular among young readers.

The Challenges of ADHD and Dyslexia

One of the most distinguishing features of Pilkey's childhood was his struggle with Attention Deficit Hyperactivity Disorder (ADHD) and dyslexia. These conditions were less well understood in the 1970s than they are now. Children who showed signs of hyperactivity, difficulty focusing, and difficulties with reading and writing were frequently labeled as troublemakers rather than being identified as having learning disabilities.

With ADHD, Pilkey found it difficult to sit through a lesson. His mind would race from one thought to the next, making it almost impossible for him to concentrate on what his teacher was saying. When the lessons became too much for him, he would fidget, doodle on his papers, and find other ways to distract himself. His teachers frequently mistook his behavior for defiance rather than an indication of his ADHD.

Furthermore, his dyslexia made reading and writing extremely difficult. Words on the page frequently appeared jumbled or out of order, making it difficult for him to keep up with his classmates. When he attempted to write, his spelling and grammar were frequently criticized, reinforcing the belief that he was simply not good at school. Tests, homework, and reading assignments all became stressors rather than opportunities to learn.

Pilkey was frequently sent to the hallway for punishment as a result of his struggles. In an era when teachers had little patience for students who did not fit the traditional mold, he was frequently excluded for being disruptive. His desk was occasionally placed outside the classroom, reinforcing the notion that he did not belong with the rest of the students. This could have crushed his spirit, but instead, it marked the unexpected start of his creative journey.

Instead of feeling defeated, Pilkey spent his time in the hallway drawing and creating stories. With nothing else to do, he began sketching funny characters and creating imaginative adventures. This is where the first seeds of "Captain Underpants" were planted. What began as a pastime quickly evolved into a passion that provided him with a sense of purpose.

Pilkey has frequently discussed how his struggles shaped him. In interviews, he has stated that he understands what it is like to be a child who does not fit in. This personal experience is what makes his books appeal to so many children today. Pilkey does more than just write stories; he writes for children who, like him, feel different, restless, or unwelcome in traditional academic settings. His books instill a sense of belonging in children, demonstrating that their creativity, wit, and distinct ways of thinking are strengths rather than weaknesses.

Finding Solace through Drawing and Storytelling

For many children, school represents structured learning and predictable routines. Pilkey used it as a backdrop for his creativity. While he struggled with reading and writing as expected by teachers, he excelled at storytelling when given the opportunity to express himself through drawing and comics.

His passion for drawing began early. He would spend hours drawing characters, inventing silly adventures, and coming up with ridiculous names that made him laugh. Unlike school assignments, which could be frustrating and rigid, drawing allowed him to express himself freely. It was his escape, a world in which he could set the rules.

His sense of humor was one of his earliest sources of inspiration. He was naturally drawn to stories that made him laugh, and he wanted to bring the same joy to others. He enjoyed the work of cartoonists such as Charles Schulz, the creator of "Peanuts" and other newspaper comic strips. These cartoons taught him that storytelling does not have to be serious; it can be funny, ridiculous, and imaginative.

It wasn't long before Pilkey began developing his own comic characters. Captain Underpants, the hero who would later become famous, was born around this time. Pilkey came up with the concept in second grade when he drew a silly superhero in underwear and a cape. His classmates found it hilarious, and their laughter inspired him to continue drawing. Even though his teachers didn't value his creative efforts, his peers did—and that was important.

Pilkey became inspired by his classmates' reactions and began creating homemade comic books, stapling pages together and sharing them with his friends. He didn't realize it at the time, but this marked the start of his career as an author and illustrator. The very abilities that made traditional schoolwork difficult—his hyperactive imagination, his need to move and create—became driving forces behind his success.

His parents, particularly his mother, were encouraging of his creativity. She encouraged him to write and draw at home, giving him the opportunity to improve his skills. Unlike his teachers, who frequently saw his doodling as a distraction, his mother saw it as something worthwhile. This encouragement helped Pilkey gain confidence in his abilities.

Pilkey's love of storytelling grew stronger with age. While school remained a challenge, he had found something that gave him meaning. His imagination became his greatest strength, and he clung to it despite his discouragement.

Years later, when Pilkey finally published "Captain Underpants", it demonstrated that the very things that got him into trouble as a child—his boundless energy, love of humor, and unconventional way of thinking—were actually gifts.

Dav Pilkey's early life was fraught with challenges that could have deterred him from achieving success. Growing up in Ohio, struggling with ADHD and dyslexia, and receiving repeated punishments at school may have led him to believe that he was incapable of achieving great things. Instead of letting those difficulties define him, he used them to fuel his creativity.

Pilkey found solace in drawing and storytelling, which led him to his true passion. His early experiences not only shaped him as a writer and illustrator, but also provided him with the empathy needed to create books that resonate with young readers, particularly those who struggle with traditional learning methods.

His childhood serves as a reminder that even the most difficult challenges in life can lead to extraordinary results. Today, millions of children enjoy his books, demonstrating that creativity, humour, and perseverance can transform challenges into opportunities.

CHAPTER 2

School Struggle and Early Inspiration

Many children view school as a place for learning, discovery, and social development. However, for Dav Pilkey, it often felt like a battleground. He was diagnosed with Attention Deficit Hyperactivity Disorder (ADHD) and dyslexia at a young age, making traditional schooling extremely challenging. His teachers expected him to sit still, concentrate on lessons, and complete assignments neatly and on time—tasks that seemed nearly impossible for him.

Instead of excelling in the structured classroom environment, Pilkey was constantly in trouble. He couldn't concentrate for long, and his hyperactive personality made him restless. His mind would wander, and he frequently found more pleasure in daydreaming or doodling than in learning the lessons. His dyslexia made it difficult for him to read, as letters appeared jumbled or out of order. Writing assignments were equally frustrating; his spelling and handwriting were frequently criticized, making him believe he would never succeed academically.

His teachers, like many others at the time, misunderstood these educational challenges. Rather than recognizing that Pilkey required alternative methods of learning, they labeled him as a troublemaker. He was often sent to the hallway as punishment for disrupting class. His desk was sometimes placed outside the classroom door, separating him from his peers. Instead of helping him, these punishments made him feel even more isolated and discouraged.

One of Pilkey's most disheartening experiences was the constant negative feedback he received. His report cards frequently mentioned his inability to focus, poor behavior, and difficulties with reading and writing. These comments reinforced the notion that he was not "smart" in the traditional sense.

Despite all of these challenges, Pilkey's imagination remained unwavering. While school was a source of frustration, it also provided the setting for his creative escape. When he was sent to the hallway, instead of feeling sorry for himself, he grabbed a pencil and began drawing.

The Creation of "Captain Underpants"

During one of these many hallway punishments, Dav Pilkey created Captain Underpants, his most famous character.

The inspiration came from his love of superheroes and his mischievous sense of humor. Traditional superheroes such as Superman and Batman were serious and heroic, but Pilkey aimed to create something ridiculous and funny. What if a superhero wore only underwear and a cape instead of a fancy costume? That idea made him laugh, and he quickly began sketching.

His classmates "loved it. The idea of a goofy superhero running around in his underwear was precisely the type of humor that children found amusing. Pilkey was encouraged by their laughter and continued to draw and develop the character. He began drawing comic strips about Captain Underpants on folded sheets of paper and stapling them together to make small homemade comic books.

Even though his teachers objected to his comics, his classmates couldn't get enough of them. Kids would pass them around, excited to see what crazy adventure Captain Underpants would embark on next. The more people laughed, the more inspired Pilkey became. He realized that despite his struggles in school, he possessed a unique talent—the ability to make others laugh through storytelling.

Captain Underpants was more than just a silly idea; it was a reflection of Pilkey's personal experiences. Pilkey's main characters, George Beard and Harold Hutchins, were two mischievous kids who enjoyed pulling pranks and drawing comics, just like him. Mr. Krupp, their school principal, was inspired by the strict and grumpy teachers Pilkey had encountered in school.

Despite his struggles in school, these comics became his lifeline. They instilled in him a sense of "purpose and confidence. Even though he didn't excel in math or reading like his peers, he did create something that made others happy. This realization shaped his career and influenced his approach to writing children's books.

Encouragement from Teachers and Family

Many of Pilkey's teachers saw him as a troublemaker, but a few recognized his potential. These teachers, rather than punishing him for his creativity, encouraged him to continue drawing and writing.

One teacher in particular stood out: a caring educator who saw past Pilkey's hyperactivity and learning difficulties. Instead of dismissing his doodles as a distraction, this teacher praised his creativity and even suggested that he consider becoming a professional cartoonist someday. This simple encouragement sowed the seed of hope in Pilkey's mind. For the first time, he realized that his artistic abilities could lead to something meaningful.

Outside of school, Pilkey's family was one of his primary sources of support. His parents, especially his mother, encouraged him to pursue his interest in storytelling. She noticed that drawing and creating comics made him happy, and rather than discouraging it, she encouraged it.

His mother would frequently give him supplies—blank paper, pencils, and crayons—and allow him to spend hours sketching. She did not put pressure on him to perform like other children who excelled in traditional academics. Instead, she let him express his creative side. She also expressed an active interest in his comics, laughing at his jokes and inquiring about his characters. This unconditional support enabled Pilkey to gain confidence in his abilities.

Even though his father was preoccupied with work, he expressed his support in small but significant ways. He would listen to Pilkey discuss his comic ideas while occasionally chuckling at his drawings. These small moments of encouragement made a significant difference in Pilkey's life.

While school remained difficult for him, knowing that he had the support of his family and a few understanding teachers encouraged him to persevere. Their encouragement gave him hope that his passion for drawing and storytelling wasn't a waste of time.

Overcoming the Odds

Despite the numerous challenges he faced, Pilkey never gave up on his passion for storytelling. Although his teachers frequently chastised him for drawing in class, he never stopped creating. Even when he was alone in the hallway, he used the opportunity to transform frustration into inspiration.

Pilkey's comic-book skills improved as he grew older. By the time he reached high school, he had created dozens of homemade comics and significantly improved his storytelling skills. He wasn't just drawing funny pictures; he was creating entire stories filled with humor, adventure, and memorable characters.

His big break came when he entered a national student writing competition while in college. He submitted one of his stories, "World War Won", and was surprised when he won first place. This victory was a watershed moment—it demonstrated that his work had real value. Winning the competition provided him with the confidence to pursue a career in children's literature.

Looking back, it's clear that Pilkey's struggles in school helped shape him into the storyteller he is today. His experiences as an outsider, dealing with ADHD and dyslexia, and getting in trouble for being overly creative all shaped his distinct voice.

Rather than being defeated by these challenges, he made them into strengths. He focused his energy on writing books that children, particularly those who feel misunderstood, could relate to. His books celebrate humor, creativity, and the power of imagination, demonstrating that sometimes your differences are what make you unique.

Today, Pilkey's books are enjoyed by millions of children worldwide. His journey from struggling student to best-selling author exemplifies the power of perseverance, creativity, and self-belief. It also serves as an inspiration for children who are facing their own academic challenges, reminding them that success does not always come from following the rules—it often comes from breaking them in the best way possible.

CHAPTER 3

College Years and the Path to Becoming An Author

After struggling in school, where his creativity was frequently misunderstood, Dav Pilkey took an important step toward his future by enrolling at Kent State University in Ohio. College was a new beginning for him, a chance to shape his identity without being labeled as a "troublemaker" or a "disruptive student."

Kent State provided an environment that was vastly different from his previous years of school. Unlike elementary and high school, where he was frequently reprimanded for doodling in class, college gave Pilkey the freedom to explore his creativity. Professors encouraged students to think independently and express themselves in unique ways, which was precisely what Pilkey required.

Pilkey studied graphic design and illustration at Kent State, where he honed his artistic and storytelling abilities. For the first time, he was surrounded by people who shared his enthusiasm for creativity. He was no longer the odd one out; he had friends and mentors who valued his skills.

One of the most significant changes in college was Pilkey's increased control over his schedule and learning process. Unlike elementary school, where he had to sit still for long hours, college allowed him to work at his own pace. He could take breaks as needed, work on projects that interested him, and spend more time honing his storytelling skills.

However, this did not mean that college was easy. Pilkey was finally in an environment where he could thrive creatively, but he still struggled academically. His ADHD and dyslexia did not go away when he started college. Reading dense textbooks remained difficult, and he often struggled to stay organized. Rather than viewing these difficulties as setbacks, he concentrated on his strengths—drawing and storytelling—and worked toward his goal of becoming an author.

First Steps to Publishing

Pilkey made a significant step in his college career when he submitted his work to a national student writing contest. He entered "World War Won", a book that he had written and illustrated. The book, a clever and humorous look at war and peace, demonstrated his ability to blend humor with meaningful themes, which would later define his career.

To his surprise and delight, he took first place in the competition. This marked a turning point in his journey. Winning the contest confirmed his belief that he possessed something unique to offer the world. For the first time, he had proof that his stories could connect with readers beyond his close circle of friends and classmates.

The contest prize was more than just an award; it included a publishing deal. This indicated that "World War Won" would be professionally published and distributed. It was Pilkey's first real step into the world of publishing, and it inspired him to keep going.

Pilkey learned valuable lessons about the industry while publishing his first book. He learned about editing, illustrating, and working with publishers, all of which would be useful skills in his future career. Most importantly, it strengthened his conviction that he could make a career out of writing and illustrating children's books.

Early Work and Rejections

Winning the contest and having "World War Won" published was a huge accomplishment, but Pilkey quickly realized that success in the publishing industry did not come easily. After his first book, he continued to write and illustrate, eager to see more of his work published. However, he soon discovered a harsh reality: rejection was a significant part of the process.

Pilkey started submitting his stories to various publishers, but the majority of them rejected his manuscripts. The reasons varied: some publishers thought his humor was too silly, others saw no market potential in his work, and some simply weren't interested. He received dozens of rejection letters, each one a painful reminder that breaking into the publishing industry was not an easy task.

At times, the rejections were discouraging. He had put a lot of effort into his stories, only to have them rejected repeatedly. Instead of giving up, Pilkey turned each rejection into motivation to improve. He improved his storytelling, adjusted his illustrations, and kept moving forward.

One of the most difficult challenges he faced was convincing publishers that his style of humor had an audience. Many publishers at the time preferred children's books with more traditional, moral-driven stories, whereas Pilkey's books featured silly jokes, mischievous characters, and over-the-top humor. What publishers didn't realize was that kids loved that kind of storytelling—they simply hadn't seen enough of it.

Pilkey worked odd jobs to support himself while writing his books, including at a pizza restaurant. He would devote his free time to writing, drawing, and submitting manuscripts, determined to break through the publishing barrier. He maintained a positive attitude, believing that if he persevered, he would eventually succeed.

After several rejections, his perseverance finally paid off. One of his early works, "Dog Breath: The Horrible Trouble with Hally Tosis", was accepted for publication. The book, about a dog with extremely bad breath, was full of Pilkey's signature quirky humor and playful storytelling. It was a hit with kids, demonstrating that there was a market for his style of writing.

Pilkey's career progressed gradually from there. He continued to write and illustrate, honing his characters and developing new book ideas. Each published book helped him get closer to his ultimate goal of becoming a full-time children's author.

The Road to Success

Pilkey's early years in publishing were fraught with setbacks, but he never let failure deter him. He saw rejection as a stepping stone to success, rather than a failure. Every rejection letter indicated that he was trying, learning, and improving.

His persistence eventually led to the creation of Captain Underpants, a character he had first imagined as a child. The character's goofy, rebellious nature reflected Pilkey's own school experiences, making the story feel both personal and relevant. However, even Captain Underpants received rejections before being published.

When "The Adventures of Captain Underpants" was released, it was an instant success. Kids enjoyed the combination of humor, action, and comic book-style storytelling. Teachers and parents were divided: some thought the book was too silly and encouraged mischief, while others saw it as an excellent way to engage reluctant readers. Despite the controversy, children couldn't get enough of Captain Underpants, and the novel quickly became a bestseller.

The success of "Captain Underpants" marked a watershed moment in Pilkey's career. He progressed from an aspiring author struggling to get published to one of the world's most popular children's book authors.

Even after achieving success, Pilkey never forgot the difficulties he encountered. He used his books to encourage students who, like him, struggled in school. He made reading enjoyable and accessible, demonstrating that you don't need to be a straight-A student to succeed.

Looking back on his life—from a child who was constantly in trouble for drawing in class to a best-selling author—it's clear that Pilkey's challenges shaped him into the writer he is today. His ADHD and dyslexia, once viewed as flaws, have become the very things that make his stories unique and relatable.

His college years served as a solid foundation for his future career. Kent State helped him improve his skills, winning the student writing contest gave him confidence, and facing rejection taught him the value of perseverance. Without these experiences, the world may not have known Captain Underpants, Dog Man, or any of the other beloved characters who have since become childhood favorites.

Finally, Pilkey's story is about determination, creativity, and never giving up on a dream. His journey to becoming an author was not easy, but his struggles made his success all the more meaningful. And his books continue to inspire children to embrace their creativity, believe in themselves, and never give up dreaming.

CHAPTER 4

A Breakthrough for Captain Underpants

Many authors, including Dav Pilkey, have found success after a long, winding road of trial and error. While he had some early success with books like "Dog Breath: The Horrible Trouble with Hally Tosis", his true breakthrough came when he created Captain Underpants, a character that would not only change his career but also revolutionize children's literature.

Pilkey didn't come up with the idea for Captain Underpants when he was older. Instead, it originated in his childhood. As a young boy with ADHD and dyslexia, he found school difficult, and one of his coping strategies was to draw silly comics to entertain himself and his classmates. He enjoyed making his friends laugh, and one of his early creations was Captain Underpants, a ridiculous, underwear-clad superhero with a bald head and a big, goofy grin.

Pilkey and his friends would pass around his homemade comics in class, laughing at Captain Underpants and his sidekicks' ridiculous adventures. However, his teachers did not find them amusing. In fact, they frequently chastised him for doodling in class rather than paying attention to the material. One teacher even ripped up his comics in front of him, telling him that he would never be able to make a living by drawing silly books.

That moment could have been discouraging, but Pilkey clung to the concept of Captain Underpants. It would be years before he returned to the character, but the seed had been planted in his mind.

Fast forward to his early days as a struggling writer, when Pilkey decided to bring Captain Underpants back to life. He realized that the humor and mischief that got him into trouble as a child were precisely what made his storytelling unique. If he liked Captain Underpants as a kid, other kids would love him too.

The Road To Publication

After Pilkey completed the story and illustrations for "The Adventures of Captain Underpants", he faced a new challenge: convincing a publisher to take a chance on it. At the time, children's books tended to follow more traditional storytelling formats, with tidy, moral-driven stories. Pilkey's book, on the other hand, was packed with cartoonish humor, flip-o-rama action scenes, fart jokes, and rebellious students who played pranks on their teachers.

Publishers were unsure whether such a book would be appropriate for children. Some people complained that the humor was too silly, while others worried that it encourages bad behavior. Pilkey received numerous rejection letters throughout his career.

But he refused to give up. He believed in his book and knew that children would love it if they had the opportunity to read it.

Finally, in 1997, Scholastic took a chance on Captain Underpants. The publishing behemoth, known for its dedication to children's literature, recognized that Pilkey's book had something unique. They recognized its potential for engaging reluctant readers, particularly children who, like Pilkey, struggled with traditional reading.

When Scholastic published "The Adventures of Captain Underpants", they gave Pilkey creative freedom, allowing him to keep the comic book-style storytelling, the amusing antics of George and Harold, and even the famous "Flip-O-Rama"—an interactive feature in which kids could flip pages back and forth to create their own animated action scenes.

The moment Captain Underpants hit the shelves, it was obvious that Pilkey had created something revolutionary.

Instant Success and Fan Reception

"The Adventures of Captain Underpants" was not just a success, but an explosion. The book flew off the shelves and quickly became a favorite among children throughout the country.

What made Captain Underpants special?

1. It was written for kids, not just parents and teachers. Unlike many traditional children's books, which frequently had a strong educational focus, "Captain Underpants" was simply fun. It spoke directly to kids in their own language, full of wit, mischief, and imagination.

2. It made reading enjoyable for reluctant readers. Many children, particularly those with ADHD and dyslexia, struggle to read because traditional books are boring or overwhelming.

"Captain Underpants" changed this. With short chapters, large text, engaging illustrations, and comic-book elements, it became the ideal book for children who did not normally enjoy reading.

3. The humor was spot on. Pilkey understood exactly what made children laugh. Every page of "Captain Underpants" was written with young readers in mind, from ridiculous character names (Professor Pippy Pee-Pee Poopypants, anyone?) to outrageous plotlines.

As soon as children began reading the book, word spread like wildfire. Parents, teachers, and librarians quickly realized that "Captain Underpants" was more than just a silly book; it was also getting kids to read. Many children who had previously struggled with reading devoured Pilkey's books, eager to see what trouble George and Harold would get into next.

As the book became more popular, Pilkey began expanding the series, creating sequels that introduced even more wild characters and hilarious adventures. "Captain Underpants and the Attack of the Talking Toilets" and "Captain Underpants and the Perilous Plot of Professor Poopypants" were instant bestsellers.

Controversies and Challenges

Despite its success, Captain Underpants has sparked controversy. Some parents and educators expressed concern that the book's humor was too crude and might encourage children to misbehave at school. Indeed, the series became one of the most frequently challenged and banned books in schools and libraries throughout the United States.

Critics argued that the book promoted disrespect for authority, encouraged pranks and bad behavior, and contained inappropriate humor. Some schools even attempted to completely ban the books, fearing that they would have a negative impact on children.

But Pilkey stood by his work. He believed that humor was a powerful tool for engaging young readers, and he argued that books should be fun rather than educational. He pointed out that the books did not promote bad behavior, but rather celebrated creativity, friendship, and imagination.

Pilkey's response to the controversy was straightforward: if kids were reading and enjoying books, that's all that matters.

The Cultural Phenomenon

Over time, Captain Underpants became a cultural phenomenon. The books sold millions of copies worldwide, were translated into dozens of languages, and remained on bestseller lists for years.

The series' popularity resulted in:

- **Merchandise:** toys, games, and costumes.

- DreamWorks Animation produced a major animated film in 2017.
- The Epic Tales of Captain Underpants", a Netflix TV series, introduced the characters to a new generation of young viewers.

Despite the difficulties he encountered along the way, Pilkey had proven his doubters incorrect. Captain Underpants was no longer just a classroom doodle; it was one of the most popular children's book series of all time.

The success of "Captain Underpants" transformed Dav Pilkey's career, establishing him as one of the most influential children's authors of his time.

More importantly, it shifted people's perspectives on children's books. Pilkey's work demonstrated that humor, comics, and creativity could be equally important as traditional storytelling. His books inspired countless children, particularly those who, like him, struggled with reading, to discover a love for books.

Dav Pilkey's breakthrough with "Captain Underpants" was more than just a personal victory; it was a triumph for every kid who has ever felt out of place in school, struggled with learning difficulties, or simply wanted to read something fun.

His journey from troublemaking student to bestselling author demonstrates that the very things that get you in trouble as a child can also make you great as an adult.

CHAPTER 5

Overcoming Obstacles in the Publishing Industry

Dav Pilkey's success with "Captain Underpants" and other works was not without its challenges. In fact, one of the most difficult challenges he faced was censorship. While many authors aspire to see their books on bestseller lists, Pilkey's books were frequently featured on another list: the American Library Association's list of most challenged books.

Since "Captain Underpants" became a bestseller, it has been the target of book bans in schools and libraries across the United States. Critics argued that the books were inappropriate for children, citing concerns about:

- Toilet humor and crude jokes

- Mischievous behavior exhibited by the main characters, George and Harold
- Disrespect toward authority figures, such as school principals and teachers
- Mature themes, including the revelation that one of the characters, Mr. Krupp's future self, was gay ("Captain Underpants and the Sensational Saga of Sir Stinks-A-Lot")

Despite these objections, "Captain Underpants" remained extremely popular among children. However, this did not deter concerned parents and school boards from attempting to ban the series. Many schools removed the books from their libraries, and some teachers refused to include them on classroom reading lists.

Pilkey, however, did not back down. While he recognized that parents had the right to choose what their children read, he believed that kids should be free to explore books that interest them. He also saw the irony in banning books written specifically for reluctant readers—children who frequently struggled to find books they enjoyed.

One of the primary reasons "Captain Underpants" was censored was its irreverent humor and portrayal of rebellious children. Some adults were concerned that these books would encourage children to disobey authority or act out at school. However, Pilkey argued that humor was a powerful tool for engaging young readers and that "Captain Underpants" was ultimately about friendship, creativity, and doing the right thing—even if it meant bending the rules slightly.

Instead of being discouraged by the bans, Pilkey used them as motivation to continue writing books that children enjoyed. He was a firm believer that children's literature should be entertaining and engaging, rather than simply educational.

Critics vs. Young Readers' Love of His Work

Pilkey's books were criticized not only by censors, but also by literary critics and educators, who dismissed his work as lowbrow or lacking literary value. Some saw "Captain Underpants" and his subsequent works, such as "Dog Man" and "The Adventures of Ook and Gluk", as nothing more than funny, joke-filled stories with no deeper meaning.

However, young readers disagree completely.

For millions of children around the world, Pilkey's books were more than just entertaining; they were a gateway into the world of reading. Children who had previously struggled with reading—whether due to dyslexia, ADHD, or simply a lack of interest in traditional literature—found Pilkey's stories irresistible.

One of the primary reasons for this was his distinct approach to storytelling.

- Short, fast-paced chapters for easy reading

- Comic-style illustrations to break up long sections of text
- Hilarious and absurd plotlines that kept kids engaged
- Relatable characters who, like many children, found school boring but had vivid imaginations.

Pilkey wasn't writing books to win prestigious literary awards; he was writing books that kids would actually enjoy reading. And in that sense, he was extremely successful.

Some educators dismissed his work, but many teachers and librarians recognized its true value. Instead of focusing on whether his books were "sophisticated" enough, they emphasized how Pilkey's stories helped hesitant readers build confidence.

Over time, even his critics had to admit that Pilkey had accomplished something extraordinary. His books were not just popular; they inspired children to fall in love with reading, which was a far greater accomplishment than simply writing "serious" literature.

Standing firm on creative freedom

One of the most impressive aspects of Dav Pilkey's career is his unwavering commitment to creative freedom. Despite facing criticism, censorship, and industry skepticism, he never let these obstacles influence how he wrote his books.

This dedication was especially noticeable in the way he:

1. Refused to censor his humor: Pilkey never toned down his stories to make them more "acceptable" to adults. He knew that children enjoyed silly jokes, so he continued to incorporate puns, slapstick humor, and absurd characters into all of his books.

2. Defeated the significance of comics in children's literature: Many traditional publishers

and educators once dismissed comics as "not real books", claiming that they lacked the same literary value as novels. Pilkey strongly disagreed. He believed that comic-style storytelling was just as valid and important as any other type of literature, particularly for children who struggled with traditional books.

3. Promoting diverse and inclusive narratives: In later years, Pilkey made a conscious effort to include diverse characters and themes in his work. One of the most notable examples was the discovery that Mr. Krupp's future self was in a same-sex relationship, which sparked another round of controversy but also earned praise for promoting inclusivity in children's literature.

4. Encouraged children to make their own stories: Unlike many authors who concentrated solely on their own works, Pilkey actively encouraged children to write and illustrate their own stories. In interviews and public appearances, he frequently reminded young readers that they didn't need to wait until they

were adults to start creating—they could begin making their own books right away, just as he did as a child.

This philosophy of empowering young readers contributed to Pilkey's strong, loyal fan base. Kids saw him not only as an author, but as someone who understood them and encouraged them to embrace their creativity.

Power of Perseverance

If there is one thing to learn from Dav Pilkey's journey, it is that perseverance pays off.

- He was told as a child that his doodles were a waste of time, but they turned into a best-selling book series.Despite multiple rejections from publishers, he persevered in submitting his work until he was accepted.Despite criticism from educators and parents, he continued to write popular children's books.

Through it all, Pilkey stayed true to his vision. He demonstrated that books do not have to be serious to be valuable, and that the stories that make us laugh are often the ones that stay with us the longest.

An Enduring Legacy

Dav Pilkey is now recognized as a literary icon, in addition to being a successful author. His books have sold millions of copies worldwide, and he continues to write new stories to inspire young readers.

Despite the challenges he encountered in the publishing industry, Pilkey's influence on children's literature is undeniable. He did more than just write books; he changed people's perceptions of children's literature.

Through humor, creativity, and an unwavering belief in the power of storytelling, Pilkey gave kids something they desperately needed—books that made them feel seen, understood, and excited to read.

In the end, that's what really matters.

CHAPTER 6

Expanding the Pilkey Universe

Dav Pilkey's literary successes did not end with "Captain Underpants". As the series grew in popularity, Pilkey sought new creative challenges, resulting in an expansion of his literary universe. His Dog Man series captivated the world, introducing a new cast of beloved characters and cementing his reputation as a master of children's literature. Along with "Dog Man", he experimented with other works, spin-offs, and distinct artistic styles that helped him stand out in the publishing industry.

Dog Man Series' Popularity

The Birth of Dogman

Pilkey continued to develop new ideas after "Captain Underpants" became a smash hit. Dog

Man, a part-dog, part-human hero with a knack for fighting crime, was a concept he had been developing since childhood.

Dog Man originated with Pilkey's childhood doodles. Pilkey, a young student struggling with dyslexia and ADHD, frequently drew comic strips, often sketching stories that combined humor and adventure. One of those early ideas was Dog Man, a character created by the wild imaginations of George Beard and Harold Hutchins—the fictional protagonists of "Captain Underpants".

In the "Captain Underpants" books, George and Harold frequently created their own comic books, and Dog Man was one of their most beloved creations. Pilkey decided to develop this in-universe character into a standalone book series. The end result was "Dog Man", a full-length graphic novel series that quickly became a sensation.

Explosive Success and Fan Response

"Dog Man" was published in 2016 and, like "Captain Underpants", immediately resonated with young readers. The book had a simple but engaging premise:

- Dog Man, a police officer with the head of a dog and the body of a human, fights crime and battles villains
- A mix of action, humor, and heartfelt moments that appealed to both kids and parents
- Comic book-style illustrations and fast-paced storytelling, ideal for reluctant readers

The response was overwhelmingly positive. "Dog Man" quickly became a bestseller, topping the children's literature charts around the world. Schools and libraries praised the series' ability to captivate young readers, especially those who struggled with traditional novels.

What made Dog Man so appealing was its accessibility. The book contained:

- The film features humorous and exaggerated expressions, clever wordplay, fast-paced action sequences, and emotional depth as Dog Man struggles with identity, loyalty, and friendship.
- The universal themes of friendship, justice, and perseverance made the books accessible and enjoyable to children from all backgrounds.

Series Growth

The success of the first "Dog Man" book resulted in an expanding series. Pilkey published several sequels that continued the adventures of Dog Man, his allies, and enemies. Some of the most notable books in the series are:

- Dog Man: Unleashed (2017)"
- Dog Man: A Tale of Two Kitties (2017)
- Dog Man and Cat Kid (2018)

- Dog Man: Lord of the Fleas (2018)
- Dog Man: Brawl of the Wild (2019)
- Dog Man: For Whom the Ball Rolls (2019)
- Dog Man: Fetch-22 (2019)"

The books continued to dominate bestseller lists, with fans looking forward to each new installment. Pilkey had successfully expanded his literary universe beyond Captain Underpants, demonstrating that his imagination and storytelling abilities were boundless.

Spin-Offs and Other Works

As "Dog Man" gained popularity, Pilkey experimented with spin-offs and other projects. His ability to write humorous, engaging, and visually appealing stories enabled him to venture into new territories while retaining the charm that had made his previous works successful.

Cat Kid Comic Club

Cat Kid Comic Club was a highly successful spin-off of the "Dog Man" series. This series followed Li'l Petey, a beloved character from "Dog Man", as he taught a group of young frogs how to make their own comic books.

This series had a distinct meta-literary aspect because it not only entertained readers but also encouraged them to write their own stories. Pilkey's goal was to encourage children to embrace creativity and express themselves through drawing and writing, as he had as a child.

Other Books and Graphic Novels

Beyond "Dog Man", Pilkey revisited some of his earlier works, introducing them to new audiences. Some of his other notable projects are:

- The Adventures of Ook and Gluk: Kung-Fu Cavemen from the Future - A book that was later withdrawn from

publication due to racial concerns, but remained a fan favorite.
- The Dumb Bunnies: A humorous children's book series that demonstrated Pilkey's fondness for silly, absurd humor.
- Re-releases of his older works, such as "Dog Breath" and "The Paperboy", which brought his early storytelling to a new generation.

Each of these projects reinforced Pilkey's status as one of the most influential authors in children's literature.

His Unique Writing and Art Style

One of the main reasons for Pilkey's long-term success is his distinct artistic and storytelling approach. Pilkey's works differ from many traditional children's books in the following ways:

1. His Handmade and Kid-Friendly Art Style

Pilkey's illustrations are immediately recognizable. His cartoonish, hand-drawn characters appear genuine and engaging, as if they were created by a child. This makes the books more relatable to young readers and encourages them to try drawing themselves.

He deliberately avoids making his books appear too polished or overly refined, instead embracing the imperfections that make them charming and accessible.

2. Humor Appealing to Children

Pilkey understands what makes children laugh. His books contain the following:

- Puns and wordplay
- Exaggerated facial expressions and slapstick humor
- Absurd but funny situations

Rather than writing for adults, he writes for children, making certain that every joke and visual gag is tailored to what young readers find funny.

3. A Combination of Action and Emotion

Pilkey's books are lighthearted and funny, but they also contain powerful emotional moments. Characters like Dog Man, Li'l Petey, and George and Harold face real struggles, which include:

- Identifying one's place in the world
- Overcoming self-doubt
- Managing friendships and family relationships

This balance of humor and heart is one of the main reasons why Pilkey's books continue to be popular with both children and adults.

4. Empowering Children to Create

Above all, Pilkey's works inspire children to become storytellers themselves. His books frequently include sections where he teaches children how to draw characters, make their own comics, and write their own stories. This has encouraged thousands of young readers to discover their own creativity.

A Literary Universe That Continues to Grow

Pilkey's influence on children's literature continues to grow. "Dog Man", "Cat Kid Comic Club", and his numerous other works have created a vast literary universe that entertains and inspires young minds all over the world.

With each new book, Pilkey pushes the boundaries of children's storytelling, demonstrating that books can be enjoyable, engaging, and life-changing for young readers.

And as long as kids keep reading, laughing, and creating, Dav Pilkey's literary universe will expand—one hilarious, action-packed story at a time.

CHAPTER 7

Personal Life and Inspiration

Dav Pilkey's journey as a writer and illustrator is inextricably linked to his personal experiences. His struggles with ADHD and dyslexia, his childhood love of drawing, and his family's support all influenced his career. Aside from his literary accomplishments, Pilkey is a devoted husband, a passionate advocate for children's literacy, and a philanthropist dedicated to giving back to the community.

Marital and Family Life

A Private and Supportive Life

Despite being one of the most well-known names in children's literature, Dav Pilkey prefers to keep his personal life private. However, one of the most well-known aspects of his personal life is his close relationship with his wife, Sayuri Pilkey. Sayuri, who is of Japanese descent, has been a pillar of support throughout his professional life.

The couple met years before Pilkey rose to national prominence, and their relationship has been one of mutual respect and encouragement. Sayuri has played an essential role in managing his career, assisting with book tours, coordinating his public appearances, and ensuring that Pilkey maintains contact with his audience.

The Contribution of His Wife to His Career

Sayuri's presence in Pilkey's life has positively influenced his work ethic and creative freedom. Unlike some authors who struggle with the pressures of fame, Pilkey has managed his success with a strong support system at home. His wife has encouraged him to stick to his fun, creative, and humorous storytelling while also pushing him to try new ideas.

One of the most important aspects of their relationship is their shared passion for travel and culture. The couple spends a lot of time in Japan, where Pilkey draws inspiration for his novels. This international perspective has allowed him to connect with a broader audience, as his books are popular not only in the United States but also in many countries around the world.

How His Marriage Impacts His Writing

Although Pilkey does not write explicitly about his personal relationships, his books frequently include themes of love, friendship, and support. His characters, such as George and Harold from "Captain Underpants" and Li'l Petey from "Dog Man", demonstrate strong friendships and a sense of loyalty, which may be influenced by Pilkey's own close relationships.

Furthermore, Pilkey's stories frequently emphasize the importance of encouragement, which reflects the support he receives from his wife and loved ones. Just as his wife has helped him stay focused and creative, many of his books feature characters who uplift and inspire one another.

How Personal Experiences Affect His Stories

Child Struggles with ADHD and Dyslexia

One of the most distinguishing features of Pilkey's storytelling is its influence by his childhood struggles with ADHD (Attention-Deficit/Hyperactivity Disorder) and dyslexia. As a child, Pilkey frequently felt alienated in the classroom and unable to keep up with traditional teaching methods.

- He was frequently sent out of the classroom due to disruptive behavior.
- Teachers and school administrators did not understand how to manage his enthusiasm and creativity.
- He was informed that he would never succeed as a writer.

Instead of giving up, Pilkey found solace in drawing and storytelling. The same thing that got him in trouble—creating comics—became his lifeline.

Many of Pilkey's characters are inspired by his own life experiences. George and Harold, the mischievous protagonists of "Captain Underpants", represent children who struggle in traditional school environments but flourish creatively. These characters remind children that their differences can be strengths, not weaknesses.

Finding Humor in Life's Challenges

Another significant influence on Pilkey's work is his ability to turn adversity into humor. His books contain the following:

- Silly, absurd humor is appealing to children.

- Unconventional heroes who overcome their flaws.
- Themes of perseverance, in which characters face obstacles but never give up.

Pilkey's ability to make fun of his own childhood struggles has struck a chord with readers. Many children with ADHD or dyslexia see themselves in his stories and are comforted to know that someone like them became a successful author.

Adding Real-Life Inspiration to His Books

Aside from his childhood struggles, Pilkey draws inspiration from everyday life. Examples include:

- Dog Man began as a childhood comic created by him and was later expanded into a full-fledged book series.
- Captain Underpants was inspired by a joke Pilkey told in second grade,

- His love of pets and animals is a recurring theme in his writing. Many of his characters, including Petey the Cat and Dog Man, demonstrate strong human-animal bonds.

Pilkey's books continue to connect with children across generations because they use real-life experiences that make them feel authentic and relatable.

Giving Back: Philanthropic and Literacy Advocacy

Pilkey is passionate about promoting literacy and making books accessible to all children, having struggled with reading in the past. Over the years, he has donated millions of books, supported literacy programs, and collaborated with educational organizations.

Donating Books to Schools and Libraries

Pilkey believes that every child, regardless of background, should have access to books. He has partnered with nonprofits, schools, and public libraries to donate:

- Distribute thousands of copies of "Dog Man" and "Captain Underpants" to underprivileged schools.
- Provide financial support to programs that encourage children to develop a love of reading.
- Resources for schools that require books for special education programs.

For children with learning disabilities, Pilkey's books provide an entry point into reading. The use of humor, illustrations, and simple text allows children to develop literacy skills in a fun and engaging way.

Supporting Children's Literacy Organizations

Pilkey has collaborated with several organizations that focus on children's literacy and education, including:

- First Book: A non-profit that gives books to children in need.
- Reading Is Fundamental (RIF): is an organization that promotes literacy in low-income families.
- The American Library Association (ALA): Pilkey frequently speaks at library events to inspire young readers and highlight the value of books.

Through these partnerships, Pilkey has helped millions of children gain access to books that they would not have had otherwise.

Advocate for Creative Freedom

Another important aspect of Pilkey's philanthropy is his support for creative freedom. He has spoken out against book censorship, arguing that children should have access to books that both entertain and inspire them.

- Because of his witty and unconventional storytelling, many of his books have been challenged or banned in certain schools.
- Pilkey believes that children should be allowed to read whatever they want, as long as it promotes literacy.
- He actively supports libraries and educators in their fight against censorship.

His advocacy ensures that children are free to explore books without undue restrictions.

The Legacy of Inspiration

Dav Pilkey's personal life is more than just a backdrop for his work; it is the foundation of his success. His struggles, experiences, and relationships have all influenced the stories he tells and the impression he leaves on young readers.

Pilkey's marriage, personal challenges, and philanthropy have created a legacy that goes beyond books. He is more than just a writer; he is an advocate for children, creativity, and the power of storytelling.

By giving back to the community and remaining true to his passion, Dav Pilkey has ensured that his books will continue to inspire generations of young readers for years to come.

CHAPTER 8

Dav Pilkey's Legacy and Enduring Impact

Dav Pilkey's journey from a struggling student with ADHD and dyslexia to a globally recognized author and illustrator exemplifies perseverance, creativity, and the power of storytelling. His books have inspired millions of children, particularly those who feel out of place in traditional school environments. Pilkey's legacy goes far beyond the pages of "Captain Underpants" and "Dog Man"; he reshaped children's literature, championed creative freedom, and instilled a lifelong love of reading in young readers.

In this chapter, we look at Pilkey's awards and recognitions, his influence on future generations, and what the future holds for this beloved author.

Awards and Recognition

Honoring A Literary Icon

Dav Pilkey has received numerous awards and recognition for his contributions to children's literature. While his books are occasionally controversial due to their unconventional humor and storytelling, the overwhelming popularity among young readers has cemented his place as one of the most influential children's authors of all time.

Some of his most notable awards are:

- **Caldecott Honor (1997):** Pilkey received this prestigious award for his book "The Paperboy", which demonstrated his ability to write heartwarming and visually stunning stories outside of his typical humorous style.
- Disney Adventures Kids' Choice Awards: Several "Captain Underpants" books

received these awards, demonstrating their popularity among young readers.

- The Milner Award for Children's Literature (2016): This award, presented by young readers in Atlanta, recognized Pilkey's contributions to children's literature.
- **Nickelodeon Kids' Choice Awards:** Pilkey's books have received numerous reader-voted awards, demonstrating his strong connection with children.
- The New York Times Bestselling Author: Many of his books, particularly those in the "Dog Man" and "Captain Underpants" series, have topped the "New York Times" bestseller list for weeks or months at a time.

Pilkey's recognition goes beyond formal awards. Teachers, librarians, and parents frequently compliment his books on making reading enjoyable and accessible to reluctant readers. His books serve as a gateway to independent reading and are used in literacy programs, book fairs, and classrooms around the world.

Critical and popular acclaim

Despite some criticism from some educators and parents about the "immature" humor in his books, Pilkey has consistently received widespread praise from child psychologists, literacy experts, and educators for engaging children in reading.

- His books bridge the gap between struggling readers and a love of literature, particularly for children with ADHD and dyslexia.
- Pilkey's use of humor, illustrations, and relatable characters makes reading more accessible and enjoyable for children.
- Research has shown that children who struggle with traditional texts find Pilkey's books easier to read, which improves their literacy skills.

While awards and critical acclaim are important, Pilkey's greatest recognition comes from the millions of children who eagerly await his next book.

inspiring future generations

Encouraging Young Readers

Perhaps Pilkey's most profound impact is his ability to encourage children to read for pleasure. Unlike traditional educational books, his stories are written with the child's perspective in mind—they are entertaining, engaging, and never feel like a chore.

- Pilkey's work has inspired many children who previously disliked reading to fall in love with books.
- His stories demonstrate that books can be enjoyable, not just something assigned in school.
- Parents and teachers frequently report that children who previously struggled with

reading are eager to pick up a Pilkey book.

Pilkey's books offer a sense of belonging to children who identify as "class clowns" or "misfits." His characters, such as George and Harold from "Captain Underpants" and Dog Man from his more recent series, demonstrate that creativity, humor, and perseverance are just as important as traditional academic skills.

Inspiring young writers and artists

In addition to encouraging reading, Pilkey has inspired countless young readers to become writers and illustrators themselves.

- After reading "Captain Underpants" and "Dog Man", many children write their own comic books and stories.
- Schools and libraries frequently host "Create Your Own Comic" contests based on Pilkey's works.

- Some young artists have gone on to be professional illustrators and writers, citing Pilkey as an inspiration.

Pilkey has even taken steps to actively encourage children's creativity.

- He frequently hosts workshops and book tours, teaching children how to create their own characters.
- He developed interactive drawing and writing activities that allow children to participate in storytelling.
- His books frequently include blank comic pages, encouraging young readers to create their own stories.

Pilkey had an impact not only on what children read, but also on what they created. His books inspired a new generation of storytellers, demonstrating that reading is only the beginning of a lifelong creative journey.

What's Next for Dav Pilkey?

The Future of Dogman and Other Works

While "Captain Underpants" is still Pilkey's most popular series, "Dog Man" has taken on a life of its own. The series has grown significantly, with multiple bestsellers and new titles released almost annually.

- Pilkey has hinted at more Dog Man books in the future, which will follow the adventures of Dog Man, Li'l Petey, and the rest of the gang.
- Given Dog Man's immense popularity, it is likely that the series will expand into new formats, such as animated shows or movies.
- Pilkey has also produced spin-offs, such as "Cat Kid Comic Club", which focuses on young kittens discovering the power of creativity.

With so much momentum, Pilkey is expected to continue developing stories that capture the imaginations of young readers.

Expanding His Philanthropic Efforts.

Pilkey's philanthropic and literacy advocacy efforts grow in tandem with his success.

- He continues to donate books and support literacy programs for children with learning disabilities.
- Pilkey has expressed an interest in expanding global literacy efforts, which would provide children in various parts of the world with access to books.
- His fight against book censorship and bans remains a critical component of his mission.

Pilkey's future is likely to include not only new books, but also initiatives to ensure that all children, regardless of background, have the opportunity to enjoy reading.

A Permanent Impact on Children's Literature

Even as new authors emerge, Pilkey's impact on children's literature will last for decades.

- His writing style has paved the way for more graphic novels and illustrated books geared toward young readers.
- Many contemporary children's authors credit Pilkey as an inspiration for combining humor and heart in storytelling.
- The success of "Captain Underpants" paved the way for books that embrace silly, creative, and unconventional storytelling.

Even if Pilkey stopped writing today, his impact would last for generations. His books are more than just stories; they are fundamental pieces of childhood for millions of readers around the world.

A Legacy that Lives On

Dav Pilkey's story is about more than just literary success; it's about overcoming adversity, embracing creativity, and inspiring young minds. Pilkey's journey from struggling in school to becoming one of the world's most beloved authors demonstrates that differences should be celebrated rather than suppressed.

His awards, influence on future generations, and ongoing passion for storytelling establish him as a legend in children's literature. Pilkey's work will endure as long as there are children in need of a book that makes them laugh, feel understood, and sparks their imagination.

Whether through "Captain Underpants", "Dog Man", or future projects, Dav Pilkey's influence will continue to shape young readers for years to come.

CONCLUSION

Dav Pilkey's contribution to children's literature is nothing short of revolutionary. He has won the hearts of millions of young readers worldwide with his imaginative storytelling, engaging characters, and fearless writing style. His works are more than just books; they are portals into the minds of children who yearn for adventure, humor, and a sense of community.

One of the most impressive aspects of Pilkey's legacy is that his stories continue to captivate new generations of readers. Even decades after the first "Captain Underpants" book was published, children still eagerly pick up his books, drawn to his signature blend of wit and emotion. The ability to write stories that are timeless is a sign of a truly great author, and Pilkey has demonstrated this talent on numerous occasions.

His influence goes beyond the pages of his books. Pilkey's openness about his struggles with ADHD and dyslexia has made him a beacon of hope for children facing similar challenges. He has demonstrated that having a learning disability does not prevent one from achieving greatness. Instead, he has reframed these challenges as distinct strengths that have fueled his creativity and storytelling abilities.

A Role Model for Young Readers and aspiring Authors

Dav Pilkey's journey from struggling student to world-renowned author is an inspiring example of perseverance, creativity, and self-acceptance. His story inspires children to embrace their individuality and turn obstacles into opportunities. He has become a role model for both young readers who enjoy his books and aspiring writers who want to share their own stories with the world.

One of Pilkey's most powerful messages is the importance of believing in oneself. He was repeatedly told that his drawings and stories were distractions rather than talents. Nonetheless, he never let the criticisms define him. Instead, he persisted in his creation, overcoming any obstacles that arose. This is a lesson that both children and adults can learn: success comes to those who persevere in the face of doubt from others.

Furthermore, Pilkey has demonstrated that stories have the power to transform lives. Many children who struggled to read discovered joy and confidence in his books. By making reading enjoyable, he has helped countless children develop a lifelong love of literature. His books have also encouraged creativity in young readers, inspiring them to draw, write, and imagine their own worlds.

Beyond storytelling, Pilkey's generosity and advocacy for literacy have bolstered his standing. He has supported numerous literacy programs, donated books to schools and libraries, and used his platform to promote children's reading habits. His dedication to making books available to all children is yet another reason why his legacy will last.

When we consider Dav Pilkey's incredible journey and long-term impact, one thing becomes clear: he is more than just a best-selling author. He is an advocate for young readers, a pioneer in children's literature, and an inspiration to anyone who has ever felt different. His ability to connect with children on such a deep level guarantees that his books will be treasured for generations.

Pilkey's work demonstrates how humor and heart can coexist. He has created characters that children adore and stories that leave an indelible impression. Whether through "Captain Underpants", "Dog Man", or any of his other works, he has told the world stories that entertain, uplift, and inspire.

Dav Pilkey's books will remain popular as long as there are children who enjoy laughing, dreaming, and exploring the limitless world of imagination. His legacy is one of joy, resilience, and the limitless power of creativity—a lasting gift to young readers everywhere.

APPENDIX

Dav Pilkey's contribution to children's literature is undeniable. His storytelling, comedic style, and memorable characters have left an indelible impression. In this appendix, we'll look at a complete list of Dav Pilkey's books, some fun facts and trivia about his life and work, and finally recommended resources for young writers who might be inspired by Pilkey's creative journey.

List of Dav Pilkey's books

The Captain Underpants series

1. Captain Underpants and the Attack of the Talking Toilets (1999)
2. Captain Underpants and the Invasion of the Incredibly Naughty Cafeteria Ladies from Outer Space (1999).
3. Captain Underpants and the Preposterous Plight of the Purple Potty People (2000)

4. Captain Underpants and the Wrath of the Wicked Wedgie Woman (2001)
5. Captain Underpants and the Big, Bad Battle of the Bionic Booger Boy (2002)
6. Captain Underpants and the Revolting Revenge of the Radioactive Robo-Boxers (2003).
7. Captain Underpants and the Perilous Plot of Professor Poopypants (2004)
8. Captain Underpants and the Terrifying Return of Tippy Tinkletrousers (2012)
9. Captain Underpants and the Tyrannical Retaliation of the Turbo Toilet 2000 (2014).
10. Captain Underpants and the Sensational Saga of Sir Stinks-A-Lot (2015).
11. Captain Underpants and the Bombastic Battle of the Bizarre Blaarg (2016) 12. Captain Underpants and the Revolting Reversal of the Righteousness of the Really, Really, Really Big Man (2017)13. Captain Underpants and the Terrifying Tumble of the Tippy Tinkletrousers (2018).

Dogman Series

1. Dog Man (2016)
2. Dog Man Unleashed (2017)
3. Dog Man: A Tale of Two Kitties (2017)
4. Dog Man and Cat Kid (2017)
5. Dog Man: Lord of the Fleas (2018)
6. Dog Man: Brawl of the Wild (2018)
7. Dog Man: For Whom the Ball Rolls (2019)
8. Dog Man: Fetch-22 (2019)
9. Dog Man: Grime and Punishment (2020).
10. Dog Man: Mothering Heights (2021)
11. Dog Man: Twenty Thousand Fleas Under the Sea (2022)

Other works by Dav Pilkey

- The Paperboy (1996) - A story about a young boy's daily routine as a paperboy that demonstrates Pilkey's early storytelling abilities.
- World War Won (1995) - A humorous graphic novel that satirizes history, highlighting Pilkey's distinct style of combining humor and heart.

- Ricky Ricotta's Mighty Robot (1999–2017)
- Ricky Ricotta's Mighty Robot vs. the Mecha-Monkeys of Mars (1999)
- Ricky Ricotta's Mighty Robot and the Dinosaur Disaster (2000)
- Ricky Ricotta's Mighty Robot vs. the Voodoo Vultures from Venus (2001)
- Dog Breath: The Horrible Trouble with Hally Tosis (1994) - A picture book written and illustrated by Pilkey that introduces the world to his unique sense of humor.
- The Adventures of Super Diaper Baby (2002) - A spin-off of "Captain Underpants" featuring a superhero baby and his sidekick.
- Cat Kid Comic Club (2020-present) - A new series that introduces the characters from "Dog Man" to young readers interested in learning how to make their own comics.

Fun facts and Trivia(Quiz)

Here are some interesting facts and trivia about Dav Pilkey's books and life:

1. Pilkey struggled with dyslexia and ADHD:
As a child, Pilkey struggled with dyslexia and ADHD. School was difficult for him, and teachers frequently misunderstood his abilities. However, these challenges fueled his imagination, and he found solace in writing and drawing. Pilkey has stated in interviews that he was frequently sent to the principal's office for his behavior at school, but his vivid imagination and love of comic books provided him with an outlet for self-expression.

2. Inspiration for Captain Underpants:
Captain Underpants" was inspired by Pilkey's childhood love of comic books and humor. He created the characters George and Harold, which were loosely based on his own mischievous nature and a friend's personality. Their silly pranks and unwavering creativity laid the groundwork for "Captain Underpants", a

character who was more than just a superhero, but also a symbol of accepting one's quirks and imagination.

3. Pilkey's Struggles in School Were Part of His Inspiration:
The protagonists of "Captain Underpants", George and his best friend Harold, were based on Pilkey's own experiences with being labeled as "bad students." George and Harold, like many other young readers, act out in response to their frustrations with school and authority figures. Pilkey uses their characters to teach the lesson that being different is acceptable, and that everyone has something valuable to contribute.

4. Pilkey Was Inspired by His Own Sense of Humor:
Pilkey's humor is well-known for being irreverent and juvenile, but it appeals to children because it appears genuine. Pilkey has frequently stated that his sense of humor is heavily influenced by the things that made him laugh as a child, such as silly pranks, bathroom humor,

and wordplay. This is why many of his books feature characters who enjoy joking around and engaging in absurd situations.

5. The name "Captain Underpants" came from a joke made by Pilkey and his friend when they were children. They would imagine what it would be like if superheroes wore nothing but underwear, and this joke gave birth to Captain Underpants, a funny superhero character.

6. Pilkey's Books Were Translated Into Dozens of Languages:
Because of their universal appeal, Pilkey's books have been translated into more than 30 languages, making them available to children all over the world. His humorous yet heartfelt stories have impacted readers from various cultures and backgrounds.

7. Pilkey's artistic style has evolved.
Pilkey began with traditional illustrations, but over time, his art style evolved to include a simplified, comic-book aesthetic that appeals to

younger audiences. His characters are frequently drawn with exaggerated features, and his illustrations make his stories enjoyable to read and easy to follow.

8. He is a big fan of comics and graphic novels.
Pilkey cites his passion for comic books and graphic novels as a major influence on his work. He was inspired by his childhood comic books and aspired to write stories that could engage children visually and narratively. The success of his "Dog Man" series, which combines comics and traditional prose, helped to popularize graphic novels among younger readers.

Dav Pilkey Trivia Challenge!

How much do you know about the genius behind "Captain Underpants" and "Dog Man"? Take this quiz and find out!

1. What inspired Dav Pilkey to create "Captain Underpants"?
A) A comic book he read as a kid

B) A joke from his classmates in elementary school
C) His favorite superhero growing up
D) A nickname his teacher gave him

"(Answer: B A joke from his classmates in elementary school!)"

2. What condition did Dav Pilkey struggle with as a child?
A) Autism
B) ADHD and Dyslexia
C) Anxiety
D) None of the above

"(Answer: B – He had ADHD and dyslexia, which made school difficult but fueled his creativity!)"

3. What was Dav Pilkey's first published book?
A) "The Adventures of Ook and Gluk"
B) "World War Won"
C) "Super Diaper Baby"
D) "Dog Man"

"(Answer: B – "World War Won", which he wrote in college and won a contest!)"

4. What job did Dav Pilkey do before becoming a full-time author?
A) Librarian
B) Schoolteacher
C) Pizza Hut worker
D) Cartoonist for a newspaper

"(Answer: C – He worked at Pizza Hut while writing books!)"

5. What real-life event inspired "Dog Man"?
A) His childhood pet
B) A dream he had
C) A superhero comic
D) His teacher's storytelling

"(Answer: A – "Dog Man" was based on a comic he created as a kid about a half-dog, half-human police officer!)"

True or False?

6. Dav Pilkey was a straight-A student in school.
■ True
■ False

"(Answer: False! He struggled in school but found his passion in drawing.)"

7. The "Flip-O-Rama" feature in "Captain Underpants" was inspired by Dav Pilkey's love for flipbooks.
■ True
■ False

"(Answer: True! He wanted to make reading interactive and fun.)"

8. Dav Pilkey's books have never been banned.
■ True
■ False

"(Answer: False! "Captain Underpants" has been challenged and banned many times due to humor and rebellious themes.)"

9. Dav Pilkey took a break from writing to care for his aging parents.
■ True
■ False

"(Answer: True! He stepped away for a while before returning with "Dog Man".)"

10. Dav Pilkey's books are only for kids.
■ True
■ False

"(Answer: False! Many adults love his books too because of their humor and creativity!)"

Fill in the Blanks

11. Dav Pilkey's full name is _____.

"(Answer: David Murray Pilkey Jr.)"

Page | 110

12. The name of the elementary school in "Captain Underpants" is _____.

"(Answer: Jerome Horwitz Elementary School.)"

13. Dav Pilkey changed his name by dropping the letter ___.

"(Answer: "e" from "Dave" to become "Dav.")"

14. "Dog Man" was created by the characters _____ in "Captain Underpants".

"(Answer: George and Harold.)"

15. Dav Pilkey often writes near the _____ for inspiration.

"(Answer: Ocean! He loves working by the sea.)"

Match the Following

Match the Dav Pilkey book with its main character:

Book Title   Main Character

Dog Man   A) Ricky Ricotta
Captain Underpants   B) George and Harold
Ricky Ricotta's Mighty Robot   C) Petey the Cat

(Answer: 1 → C, 2 → B, 3 → A)

Odd One Out

17. Which of these is NOT a Dav Pilkey book?
A) "Dog Man"
B) "Captain Underpants"
C) "Diary of a Wimpy Kid"
D) "The Adventures of Ook and Gluk"

"(Answer: C – "Diary of a Wimpy Kid" was written by Jeff Kinney!)"

18. Which of these is NOT a character from "Captain Underpants"?
A) George Beard
B) Harold Hutchins
C) Petey the Cat
D) Mr. Krupp

"(Answer: C – Petey the Cat is from "Dog Man", not "Captain Underpants"!)"

Bonus Questions!

19. What major award has Dav Pilkey won for his books?
A) Caldecott Honor
B) Newbery Medal
C) National Book Award
D) Pulitzer Prize

"(Answer: A – The "Caldecott Honor" for "The Paperboy!")"

20. What important lesson does Dav Pilkey want kids to learn from his books?

A) That school is boring
B) That comics are fun
C) That being different is okay and creativity has no limits
D) That superheroes don't wear capes

"(Answer: C – He encourages kids to embrace their creativity and be themselves!)"

Recommended Resources For Young Writers

For young readers and aspiring writers inspired by Pilkey's stories, here are some useful resources to help them get started:

Books About Writing and Creativity

1. "Writing Magic: Creating Stories That Fly" by Gail Carson Levine.
This book is an excellent introduction to writing for young readers, with practical advice on how to write stories, develop characters, and structure plots in a fun and approachable manner.

2. "The Elements of Style" by William Strunk, Jr. and E.B. White
This classic book is ideal for anyone who wants to improve their writing style. While it may appear advanced to younger readers, it is an excellent resource for improving clarity, conciseness, and grammar in writing.

3. "How to Write a Story" by Kate Messner.
This resource is an excellent starting point for children who want to learn the fundamentals of story writing, from creating characters and settings to developing plots and themes.

4. "The Art of Comic Book Drawing" by Maury Aaseng.
Aspiring illustrators will benefit from this comprehensive guide to drawing comics. It provides step-by-step instructions for creating comic book characters, designing panels, and visually communicating stories.

Online Writing Community

- **NaNoWriMo (National Novel Writing Month):** NaNoWriMo offers an excellent program for young writers called the NaNoWriMo Young Writers Program. This initiative encourages young writers to improve their skills by setting goals and participating in a month-long writing challenge.
- **Story Bird:** Storybird is an online platform that allows young writers to create their own illustrated stories, making it an ideal tool for aspiring authors looking to try their hand at both writing and illustration.

Writing Workshops and Camps

- **Writing workshops:** Many local libraries, schools, and community centers provide writing workshops for children and teenagers. These workshops encourage creativity, improve writing skills, and allow young writers to share their work in a supportive setting.

- **Summer Writing Camps:** Summer writing and storytelling camps offer immersive experiences for young writers to hone their skills and develop their author voice. Check out local options or programs for teens, such as Writers' Workshop Summer Camp.

This appendix highlights a wide range of Dav Pilkey's works, fun facts about his career, and recommended resources to encourage young readers to begin writing. Pilkey's books have not only entertained, but also inspired young minds to embrace their creativity, just as he did as a child. For those inspired by Pilkey's storytelling, these resources can help kickstart a lifelong journey of creative expression.

Enjoyed the book?

If "Dav Pilkey Rise: How a Creative Genius Conquered Children's Literature" inspired or entertained you, I'd love to hear your thoughts!

Your review helps other readers and supports my work. It only takes a minute—just a quick rating and a few words can make a big difference!

Thank you for your support! ★

Made in United States
Troutdale, OR
05/07/2025